A ch H E G – J K Z S C – R rr D T L – ll Y ñ U O – P W B V F – N I M Q D

Concrete – Abstract: Classroom Culture from Babbling

By

Branton Burgess Baird

First edition published February 2019 by
SaintMauricePublishing
Haleyville, Alabama

Published in the United States of America

Library of Congress Cataloging-in-Publication Data: PCN 2019902778

Baird, Branton Burgess.
Concrete-Abstract: Classroom Culture from Babbling .

Includes bibliographical references and index.
ISBN: 9780998085036
1. Spanish Second Language Acquisition I. Title

SaintMauricePublishing
Haleyville, Alabama, 35565
http://www.SaintMauricePublishing.com

Sword of Destiny

Table of Contents:

Foreword

This little book explains some theory behind a teaching method that has worked in my second language classrooms. With that being said, it will not work by simply going through the motions of teaching the sound system to students and then moving onto grammar drills. The sound system must be reinforced and used throughout the class. The instructor should have native or near native pronunciation in the target language, or at least fluent production with the sound system they wish their students to develop; that is the goal. The sounds are concrete forms instead of abstract functions of any language. This book proposes is that by teaching the appropriate pronunciation and by using teaching methods that are truly communicative they will be able to come closer to native like competence. Allowing the students to build an identity by expressing themselves as a classroom community, and by using prosodic cues, built on phonetics and phonotactics, a classroom can experience extra-grammatical stimuli that most other grammar-based classrooms will not approach. This is only one step in the direction of ultimate attainment, but in my opinion, it is an important first step.

How to use this book

The letters at the top of each page in this book should produced using a Spanish sound system. Say each phoneme and then as quickly as possible proceed to the next. For an audio example please go to my youtube channel "Branton Baird." My classroom was that of beginner and intermediate Spanish at the college level, but all students improved in pronunciation and fluency, and in an ability to perceive Spanish. The letters were mixed out of order, and were produced individually and as rapidly, which made them seem like Spanish word segments. The letter "A" sounded like "ah," the letter "B" sounded like if was followed by the Spanish vowel "E," and not the English vowels. All the syllabification and resyllabification rules used in Spanish production should be used in the production of these letter streams or segments including but not limited to, lenition, hiatus, neutralization, leveling and merger, dis/assimilation, distinction, etc. In other words, try to make it sound like Spanish, or adopt this method for any other target sound system. This is an important distinction to be made, in that by using this style of production the students were required to do some linguistic (phonetic) gymnastics, which eventually led to an increased ability to perceive and produce the target language phonemes but more importantly to identify parts of speech, identify word boundaries and verb morphology, increase vocabulary and to learn sentence structures. Eventually this ability can help second language learners to identify pragmatic contexts when they differ from the intonations used in their native language.

My hope is that this book will enrich the curriculum by allowing classrooms to create a second language learning community. I believe the classroom is the perfect place to learn a second language. This method could even help with immersion scenarios if it is applied before the immersion begins. Through the use of this method I hope a specialized degree could be established oriented toward competence more so than literary or linguistic studies.

First Language Acquisition

Our mother's voice is the first and most outstanding language experience we have as infants, and even before. From the heightened pitches and funny faces used in a mother's speech we develop an ability to attend and interact with our society through language. Even as we develop in utero, we grow accustomed to the sounds filtered through mother's body and our amniotic fluid, and are born ready to attend to her and her particular language more so than to anyone else.

Some claim that this attention to language is innate; that a 'language instinct' is inborn. The meaning of this innateness is that whatever signals an infant can detect that consistently establish a pattern are eventually paired with contextual meanings which can be reproduced in order to express an idea to someone else. Eventually the patterns can be used creatively in order to create a new meaning altogether.

Most of the signals that we receive are from sound, as it began in the womb, and later from combinations of sound, gesture, and other visual symbols. By pairing these patterned stimuli with external stimuli we establish patterns which are ultimately reinforced through the act of communication. From the pairing of patterns and meaning, of forms and functions, we develop an ability to express conscious thoughts. The heart of this book focuses on concrete language patterns of sound in order to maximize abstract second language learning through participation.

Many scholars claim that this approach to second language learning is not worth the effort or simply impossible. Why they are skeptical is absolutely understandable. The goal, in essence, is to duplicate the processes which are hardwired into our daily lives. However, by focusing on the speech stream and the segmentation of a target language (Spanish) we are at least able to come closer to it by using the same basic techniques that a child does when they are acquiring their first language. We can learn anything measure by measure starting with the smallest basic unit associated with the target language. Practicing the sound system of a language enables the language learner to more easily attend to and participate within the language using the most basic units of the language, instead of participating with the most basic units of their native language. Superficially, this argument make sense, and as we get deeper into the benefits of learning the target language sound system, we will see that it is an easy and critical step to reach ultimate attainment in said language.

The speech stream, when uttered using target language phonemes often sounds like 'rattling' to non-speakers. That the rattling on is perceptible is a good sign that the listener can hear the differences between that and their native language, and is indicative of noticing the prosody or musicality of the language, even though some languages do not sound much like music to a native English speaker. Eventually the prosody develops into richer and more contextualized information can be adapted for speech in a second language. In order to make this work, the prosody has to be automatic in production and perception. We have to raise awareness of it to such a degree that we can then forget all about it.

Certain phonemes are acquired at earlier ages in different languages. Phonemes are not exactly uniformly acquired and developed across language cultures, or across speakers for that matter. The order of phoneme acquisition for native English speakers is different for native Spanish speakers. One major difference is the age of acquisition for the /l/ phoneme. In Spanish the /l/ phoneme is learned earlier than in English, which researchers propose is due to the frequency of occurrence in either language, as well as the higher functional load of the /l/ in Spanish than in English as was discovered in an acquisition study produced by Lorena Cataño and her colleagues. The uniformity is akin to that of a military base which has members that look the same to the casual observer, but more closely the uniforms distinguish ranks, duties, awards and varying levels of formality. Training the ear of the second language student is not all that using this method can do; fundamentally it is the basis for creating a different mindset to language learning in the classroom.

The mindset of our native language is developed very early, and is spurred by an infant's curiosity. Imagine that a scientist has discovered a way to give every person 100 billion unused neurons, and realize just how curious a pre-natal infant or a new born must be about their environment. It is not that we would automatically be smarter, we would be 100 billion times more motivated to learn and we would have the extra neurons to create connections that we want. Even without the extra 100 billion neurons, we can experience the joy of discovery every time we learn something new, or when we figure out the solution to a vexing problem. It is not simply a reduction in emotional stress (distress), which comes from solving a problem that is pleasurable. By creating a solution to a problem we have neurologically connected two areas that had not been previously connected. This connectivity is not without its cost, however, and we will have to rest and perhaps even to rehearse the solution again in order to make sure we problem solve the same way in the future. This rehearsal is less and less rewarding to us by the time we finally solve the problem. The novelty wears of, and the learning gets old. At this point we may actually use the sound system automatically.

The process of the old lessons getting old is called habituation. Without habituation we would be constantly engrossed in the same lessons over and over again. The joy of discovery discussed above is the opposite of habituation, we call it sensitization. The more reliably a stimulus is paired with neuronal activation of any kind determines which functions become sensitized. These functions become so easily activated as to make them automatic. The things we learn that cause a spark in our minds become easier to stimulate until they reach the point that it is no longer "exciting" to activate i.e. habituation. By using the syllabification of Spanish we are able to sensitize and then habituate its sound structure and in doing so we are able to perceive the language more clearly. This process of sensitization and habituation will allow us to hear more nuanced meaning, and could also facilitate the ability to learn a second language similar to the way we learn our native language. We may also be emotionally motivated by the sounds we hear from a biological stand point. Angry sounds being sharp, loud and forceful will inevitably lead to tears and happy sounds being soothing, soft, and sing-song will lead to smiling and maybe some laughter.

There is no greater impact we can have on a person than the happiness we expose them to as infants, from a neurological perspective. Maybe the reason most people do not remember the impact of their parents' kindnesses is because they had no point of reference for comparison. They experience pure being. They are not reminded of past relationships by the song they are now hearing, or how they should have taken that scholarship to "Big State University" instead of staying home to get married and have children. They have nothing to compare anything else to, and so they simply experience life in its purity, for the sake of experiencing it. In this sense, they experience everything at once, and a kind of meshing of the senses and meaning combines in their heads. Eventually many embodied experiences can be linked to language; this is why we may shrug our shoulders when we say that we do not know something. Language is initially biologically influenced. Those that use language very well can express ideas that others experience as mere confusion, write poems that we understand and that reach us on a deeper level than we knew how to explain. It's not that we don't think the same things; it is that we cannot always express the same thoughts using language the way others do.

Sensitization & Habituation

Sensitization, and later habituation, is what happens when a system of neurons that have become devoted to a particular function, learn to respond to a minute stimulus. This is in contrast to what it takes for a neuron that has not been habituated to respond to a stimulus. The stimulus must be significantly greater for non-habituated neurons than for habituated neurons. When one neuron fires other neurons around it will tend to fire in the same direction and for the same purpose. So if we learn a new word or sound, that item becomes easier to activate those neurons when it is encountered. A neuron's rate of firing is influenced by the "noticability" or significance of the stimulus. If something loud happens while we are having a conversation, the louder that thing is makes it more and more difficult to ignore. This "loudness" is relative of course. A man's tie can be "loud," when it stands out or clashes with the rest of his attire. In this sense, it is simply how much the tie stands out compared to what the man is wearing and what the viewer's experience of ties allows them to claim statistically about how much they cannot ignore such an obnoxious piece of clothing. This phenomenon occurs with language as much as with any finely developed sense, however with language all first language users are pretty much experts at discerning meaning.

Patricia Kuhl (1987) claims that babies use statistical like data gathering process of language prosody, and that it seems to prime the brain for linguistic input. She states that children who are delayed in mastering the phonetic cues of their native language will take longer to master later stages of language such as speaking and reading. Prosody is the first language lesson native speakers are exposed to through infant directed speech. It is from the motherese that the child develops the phonetics. Variation of the frequencies and lengthening of pauses among other aspects facilitate comprehension by making it easier to perceive exactly when a phoneme begins and ends in comparison to the rest of the utterance. Prosody gives the child listener more time to process the information, and activates more neurons because of the extreme nature of the speech patterns. This all happens within the first week of life.

After the neonates become accustomed to the speech stream, they become aware that it is made up of smaller segments. This leads to the acquisition of phonemes, and the development of phonology, which leads to babbling. From 6-9 months a child stops being so intrigued by the prosody of their native language and begins to pick out the particular phonetic differences.

When taken as a whole we can see the development away from what could be thought of as the "Charles Schultz" effect. Before we are able to discriminate phonemes, phrase boundaries, and contrastive focus a language's prosody may sound much like adults when they are speaking to Charlie Brown and his friends. Sensitivity to phonetics and phonotactics comes after the novelty of the speech stream wears off, and the detailed elements of segmentation can be discerned. From the whole, we eventually are able to see the parts, and then we can understand how the sum of the parts works together.

Stress

Processing language begins in utero, studies have shown that newborns are able to discriminate their own mother's voice from that of other females (Moon, Lagecrantz, Kuhl, 2013) they are also able to discriminate their own native tongue from nonnative languages as well. Infants are able to attend to the sounds their mother makes, and those of the other speakers in their environment, through the lining of the womb. The sounds they hear most frequently become attenuated, and beyond that we are hardwired to listen to the specific sounds of speech through the development of the auditory mechanism (Port, 2007). Interestingly, the frequencies that reach our brains first, those of higher pitch frequencies, are generally produced by females and by higher stress pitches (F0) of different utterances. Lower frequencies, representing lower tones and presumably "male" voices reach have farther to travel down the auditory mechanism. This difference may not seem like much, but to a system of billions of neurons all depending on stimulus, and weeding out "irrelevant" information, the difference is substantial.

Differences in the time it takes a signal to reach the higher frequency registers and the lower frequency registers determine what a first language learner will be able to attend. Attention determines awareness which in turn influences learning and acquisition. Schmidt claims that learners who "notice the most learn the most" (1990). The differences between learning and acquisition will be discussed in more detail later, but for the sake of noting it here learning and acquisition may represent only varying levels of directed attention. Directing attention may in truth be the most important role for an educator, instead of lecturing, which tends to bludgeon attentive minds into a coma. However, it seems that for the sake of language that our brains, ears, as well as other biological and physical functions lend themselves to directing attention toward conventional linguistic patterns. The point at which the speech signal ceases to be merely a sound and becomes language is not exactly clear either, as it may vary from child to child, language to language, and of course when the researchers or interested parties are actually paying attention enough and to the right stimuli to notice the difference.

What we are attending to as infants and what we attend to as adult learners of language seem to be the major difference in the learning/acquisition. Adults usually attend to meaning of words as semantic units carrying meaning, or to morphology (Van Patten 1985, 1987, in Schmidt 1990), having long given up on pronunciation as meaningless code. Children who are learning/acquiring a native language from which they have no definitions of any kind from which to associate to any ideas they may be having. What even is an idea for that matter? What are the boundaries of thought or ideation? Is it enough to be curious about something to make that curiosity an idea, the idea of questioning? It seems that it is sufficient, and necessary for the definition of thought to label what is thinking, and to know if language is a necessary component for thinking, as well as how language influences thinking overall. We must first discuss the emergence of language and the influences that the stimuli that govern the emergence of language continue to influence cognition throughout language use.

Vocalizations produced by infants are often loud at the moment of birth, and when crying. These sounds are functional to arouse the attention of parents, but what the infants also discover is that the sounds that their parents make also arouse their attention. It is this attention to their mother's, or parents', speech that gives the stimulus for infants to develop into language users. The language speech signal is merely a systematic pattern of interruptions of the natural vocalizations produced by all speakers with statistically average developmental patterns. With 20 weeks of age an infant's brain has developed the ability to imitate non-babbling, language specific frequencies of vowels. From six months to a year this ability becomes even more noticeable in the child's behavior, but Imada, Zhang, Cheour, Taulu, Ahonen, & Kuhl, 2006 have studied the brains of developing children through magneto encephalography (MEG) which clearly demonstrate areas of neuronal activation in the temporal lobe of the left hemisphere and motor-sensory cortex, which become more salient within the first year. This study measured the brain's responses to tonal, harmonic, and syllable stimuli produced by adults. The development demonstrates a clear pattern of neuronal development to these stimuli, demonstrating that the innateness of language is the ability to attend to these signals and to use these neuronal formations to further facilitate language development.

The point which the language emerges from the naturally produced yet not systematically linguistic sounds of an infant is hard to point to precisely, as the inherent sounds we produce will always influence linguistic structure and meaning. However, a threshold must exist that distinguishes grammar from non-grammar, and connectionist theories along with the theory of universal grammar attempt to find this moment in each of its instantiations. Stress, or the frequency, duration, and amplitude of a vocal signal becomes interrupted and modified by varying degrees of manners and points of articulation in the oral cavity as well as sonority or muteness. Overall, however, first language users demonstrate the total occlusion, obstruents or what are called 'stops' in English, are usually the first recognized signs of the emergence of systematic language. In both Spanish and English these sounds include voiced and voiceless stops, /p/ /t/ /k/, /b/ /d/ /g/ (Cataño, Barlow, Moyna, 2009). This study evaluated the phonemic acquisition order of 16 Spanish speaking children and compared the results to similar studies of English phonemic acquisition. The results clearly demonstrate that the initial phonemes acquired, or developed, by children are the aforementioned stops/occlusives, being followed by nasals, laterals, fricatives, and liquids. The farther away from the infantile stages of language acquisition we see more and more language specific patterns of development, statistically speaking. This is not surprising, however even with in each language children's development does not always follow a specific pattern. InPaula FIkkert's dissertation on the acquisition of prosodic structure (1994) demonstrates that first language acquisition of Dutch also follows the initial stages of stops. The next phoneme to be used by Dutch children is that of /h/ but Fikkert is hesitant to label this as linguistic, as at other stages of the developmental process the children will revert to its use when they have not acquired a phoneme at a higher difficulty rating of production.

The levels of difficulty of phonetic articulation and therefore phoneme acquisition, I propose, can be compared to the difficulty it takes to learn slurring in music. For example while playing a trumpet and starting at a low C it is easier to follow through the scale and stop with the high C than it is to simply start at low C and immediately 'slur' all the way to the top of high C. This difficulty is heightened when actually trying to perform a musical piece. Such articulatory development is the same in language development. Learning simply to produce the sounds that everyone else is producing, to the satisfaction of the speaker, takes a great deal of time.

The familiar patterns of total occlusion being the first phonemes acquired by children in English, Spanish, and Dutch, and probably most other languages, insinuates that the stopping of the speech signal raises awareness sudden stopping of the speech signal heightens awareness of the child. This may be the origin for the universal consonant vowel (CV) syllable structure. The phonological working memory may then recall the sound for immediate or later production for mimesis. The frequencies of vowels however, may also require some development, especially in English as compared to the inventory of Spanish vowels in particular. English has more vowel variations than does Spanish, which leads to the next topic of syllable vs. stress timed languages. This is not to say that Spanish speakers learn to speak more quickly than English speakers, but only that their vowels are less tricky.

The vowels are the heart of the stress patterns in a language. Consonants can 'carry' stress, but the stress peaks are invariably over a vowel. Stress patterns help categorize languages into different groups known as stress timed, syllable timed, or mora timed languages. Stress timed languages are said to separate their words through patterns of varying stress as opposed to isochronous patterns of syllables (Gutiérrez Díez, 2001). The syllable timed languages are said to have more reliably predictable speech rates or syllable durations than stress timed languages, this predictable stress pattern is known as isochrony. (Ramus, Nespor & Mehler, 1999) explored the vowel and consonant durations and pitches of eight languages, (Catalan, Dutch, English, French, Italian, Japanese, Polish, and Spanish), establishing a continuum of syllable and stress timed languages which were then plotted graphically to compare consonant and vocalic intervals, or the onsets to the offset of each type of phoneme. Of these eight languages Japanese was added for comparison to the mora, or vowel weight, which is drastically different than that of the rest of the group, which is borne out in the study. For the purposes of analysis the Germanic languages were labeled as stress timed, and the Romance languages as syllable timed. This study analyzed three different criteria for categorizing languages due to their timing; %V the average proportion of vocalic intervals, the average standard deviation of consonantal (Delta C) and vocalic (Delta V) intervals of all language samples. With this method the researchers were able to triangulate at least these three factors relating to stress. The results did find highly significant patterns of %V and Delta C, but not Delta V. While these results demonstrate a better starting point for the timing classification of languages, a great deal of data has yet to be operationally defined let alone analyzed, and the authors indicate that the groups have less clearly defined boundaries and quite a bit of overlap exists. Stress patterns tend to group languages along a continuum of acoustic and rhythmic characteristics rather than languages being labeled into one group or another; i.e. some languages' stress patterns behave as those in other languages despite being labeled as stress timed or syllable timed.

Statistical measure of human behavior is necessary but insufficient to explain all the vagaries which turn up. For example, one might suppose that since two Romance languages share syllable timing that their interlanguage may not be influenced by this factor in the case of second language learning, however this is not the case. Dupoux, Pallier, Sebastian, Mehler (1997, 2007) demonstrated "stress deafness" in French speakers learning Spanish as a second language. In this study the participants were asked to identify the location of stressed accents in triplets. The example nonse words were presented to the participant as follows: *bOpelo – bopElo.* The participants were then presented with a third option and were asked which of the two first samples matched the third and last word with regards to stress.

The16 Parisian participants, all students aged around 25 years old, had significantly more difficulty identifying the stressed syllables than compared to the Barcelonan students. The French students had difficulty discriminating or matching the third word with either of the accented words from the stimulus.

In a second experiment of the same study (Dupoux et al. 1997) the participants were asked to ignore the stress signals and to match the X stimuli with either A or B according to phonetic segments alone. In this second experiment the Spanish participants had difficulty ignoring stress in the ABX text, whereas the French participants were better able to discriminate by phonemic segmental differences alone. The French participants were easily able to disregard the stress, and had significantly faster reaction times than the Spanish participants when focusing on the segments, and not the stress. This research concludes that different languages, even within the same family, are parameterized to process phonemes, speech rhythm, and even the relationships between the consonants and vowels at different rates, and that these processes may interfere with each other due to the first language experience, when trying to learn a second language.

The stress deafness leads to another conclusion about the differences between stress timings in languages, not that the categories of syllable timed or stress timed do not exist but that there is an element of the processing of any language that cannot be measured behaviorally and therefore statistically. All we can do is measure the stimulus, but not necessarily the response, which on one level is perception. This type of response may pit two like categories against each other and scientists and researchers will draw conclusions that are inherently fallacious about the nature of learning and acquisition. I am proposing that languages such as French have developed such a high degree of sensitivity to their own phonetic system that other languages may overstimulate the French L1 ear, or cause some other kind of linguistic blocking. The same may be true of other interlanguage varieties, but the nature of each can be counteracted if we educate the second language learner to attend to the target language's phonetic characteristics.

Each language phonetic characteristic can be quantified statistically in more specific ways by analyzing its phonotactics. More specifically within the domain of phonotactics is the category of *neighborhood density,* which is something akin to a statistical analysis of all a languages minimal pairs from a phonemic perspective. For example, the word *cat* has neighboring words includes but is not limited to the following: "*hat, fat, rat mat, sat, cut, kit, cot, can, cap, calf*" (Vitevitch & Stamer, 2006). One word in the neighborhoods of words is sometimes thought to be heard instead of the word a speaker has actually produced in what has been termed "slips of the ear" (Vitevitch, 2002b in Vitevitch & Stamer, 2006). In this study words in the same neighborhood were used to find a neighborhood density of other like words to investigate the speed of processing of similar words within a language. By using two different "neighborhoods," one sparse and one dense, the researchers were able to compare the speed of response when participants were asked to verbally identify an image in a picture naming task. The stimuli were presented and the amount of time it took the participants to response was measured later to be analyzed by an ANOVA by comparing the response times against neighborhood density and neighborhood sparsity.

Previous studies of this type investigated the influence of neighborhood density on the speed of processing English words. In Vitevitch & Stamer (2006) however, the target language of analysis was Spanish. The results of Vitevitch & Stamer (2006) indicate that English and Spanish are processed differently with regards to phonotactic structure. Spanish words with sparse neighborhood densities were responded to more quickly than words with dense neighborhood densities "In English, words with dense neighborhoods are produced more quickly than words with sparse neighborhoods." (Vitevitch, 1997, 2002b in Vitevitch & Stamer 2006).

Stress patterns are sufficient for native speakers to discriminate between their own language, and even another dialect, therefore stress plays at least a small role in the processing of language. In other words, specific language processing is not limited to the phonemes, but also the intonation patterns (Barkat, Ohala, Pellegrino 1999). Arabic speakers from four different countries (Morocco, Algeria, Syria and Jordan) were asked to record speech samples which were then modified to eliminate the segmental cues using a computer program called Matlab. The speech samples were presented to Arabic and non-Arabic speakers. The native Arabic speakers were able to discriminate between dialects using only the low pass filtered signals, yet the scores for Arabic speakers was statistically significant ($p. <.005$) to identify their own native dialect. The point is that some level of language processing occurs at the prosodic level, but it is unclear how to train this in a classroom.

Previous scholars have suggested that it is impossible to acquire or learn such linguistic features after a critical or sensitive period for language learning; however there are always exceptions to philosophical absolutes. Ineke Mennen (1989) performed a study of Dutch Speakers of Greek to analyze their peak alignment with the syllables in the target language. One participant advanced learner of Greek, from Dutch L1(DG4), was able acquire Greek peak alignment against all predictions that such a task is impossible after the critical period (CPH).

Specifically, DG4's peak alignment as a native Dutch speaker and an advanced learner of Greek matched the phonlength of Greek in short and long conditions, thereby affording her the opportunity to align her stress appropriately to her 2nd or 3rd lang. of Greek. It is mentioned earlier in Mennen (1989) that most participants spoke English. Statistical analysis of her data, using the Post-Hoc Sheffe tests to compare groups, shows that DG4's productions match the baseline Greek stress production; Group G ($p =$ ns, at the $p< 0.05$ level) and Group DG (DG4) ($p =$ ns, at the $p < 0.05$ level) (Mennen, 1989).

The Dutch native speakers had trouble with the phonlength when speaking Greek, meaning that in both long and short conditions of syllable length, the peak of their stress in F0 did not align with the peaks of their target language, matching more to their native language. Mennen (1989) proposes that the participants in her study had not "merged" the production systems from Dutch to Greek. Citing James Flege's (1995) theory of the Speech Learning Model (SLM), which concludes that in order to achieve a native-like target language production system a language learner will combine their phonetic and prosodic systems in order to facilitate target language production. Flege also holds that when learning a L2 the phonetic system of the target will influence the L1 phonetic system (1995). However it may also be possible to from the beginning of L2 learning or acquisition the L2 could be made to completely separately as though it were simply a grammatical paralinguistic form in and of itself. Logically, merging two systems may confuse the L1 production as much as the L2, and develop a non-native production in both languages. However, the ability to discriminate the sounds of two languages and to produce them as natives indicates that although the phonetic systems have been acquired, with allophones from either language fitting into the same mental space, that they may also be code-switched as if they were higher level grammatical functions. This in fact may be the case in that DG4 has actually maintained her native alignment, but also acquired Greek alignment.

Of the two conditions of this study, short and long syllables, only the short is different between the two languages. In other words, Dutch and Greek share peak alignment in long syllable conditions. Mennen (1989) concludes that the L1 peak alignment in long syllable conditions is therefore carried over to the L2, and that the short syllable conditions are too different for most of the participants to transfer. Mennen states, "At this point is not clear why it is the Dutch long (and not the short) condition which is transferred to the L2" (1989). However, this analysis seems unnecessary in that no transfer is needed if the stress patterns match, the participants may simply be using their L1 productions in order to produce L2 targets. In other words, no transfer may have occurred. This seems to be the case since in the short syllable conditions neither language aligns from the baseline comparisons. Taking possible lack of alignment from Group D to Group G, and the maintenance of DG4's peak alignment in her L1 despite acquiring L2 alignment, it seems that the systems have not merged completely, and they are compartmentalized yet connected. Some stress transfer may have occurred as the examples from all other participants in the Dutch/Greek group experienced a slight shift in their peak alignments from both their L1 and L2 categories toward each other. It may be that they are blocked from discriminating between peak alignments of either language, which then explains why noticeable but not native-like transfer has occurred (Mennen, 1989). DG4's results are most likely due to her immersion experience in Greece with the target language as compared to the rest of the participants' classroom L2 experience in the Netherlands.

Levi & Schwartz (2013) examined language specific and language-independent processing of two languages across three different age groups of young, 7-9, older young 10-12, and adults, as well as comparing the results of participants who had typical language development (TLD), and specific language impairment (SLI). All of the participants were native English speakers. The study's results suggest that as we age our ability to distinguish nonlinguistic information from the speech signal decreases. This may simply be another way of saying that the ability to discriminate non-native language characteristics fades away as we age, or a re-iteration of the (CPH) (Levi & Schwartz 2013, Lenneberg, 1967). However, this also establishes a relationship between non-native language characteristics and general acoustic perceptual abilities, indicating that there may at least be a correlation between the two. Levi & Schwartz (2013) conclude "… as listeners language skills develop, there is a trade-off between more general perceptual abilities useful for processing talker information n any language and those that are relevant to their everyday language experience and, thus tied to the phonology."

James Flege proposes that a relationship between production and perception exists in the Speech Learning Model (SLM) (Flege, 1995, 2018). This relationship is defined by the ability to accurately perceive which in turn is "translated" into the ability to produce. Perception precedes production just as in the L1. However, Fikkert (1994) demonstrates that children acquiring their L1 phonetic structures in Dutch will be able to perceive a phoneme but will be unable to produce it with adult proficiency. When a child uses a phoneme incorrectly, and is mimicked by an adult, the child will attempt to correct the adult's production while still using the inaccurate production themselves (Fikkert, 1994). Flege's SLM finds support in the order of acquisition; the perception preceding the production, however, it also implies that a difference between L1 and L2 learning and acquisition may exist.

Each language has a particular range or continuum of stimuli resulting from a modification of the speech signal in some way, which are what we call phonemes. These phonemes have thresholds of activation along various continua, or parameters, which are established by convention (Keating 2000, Lavoie 2002, Cho & Keating 2009). Establishing these conventions usually comes from our parents and our environment, but the can be learn even after the critical period as has been seen in the studies mentioned above. In order to fully acquire a second language, or even simply to facilitate the learning of it, we can learn the distinctions and when to use the phonetic systems between our 1L and our 2L. Studies have shown that even in our native language we do not always use the 'prescribed' phonetic characteristics to produce our language. This is especially true in spontaneous speech (Lavoie, 2002). The target of a /k/ in English may be modified as a stop with frication, with voicing, as an approximant, or even as a glottal fricative.

We know from previous studies that by changing the focus or emphasis of one part of speech we raise awareness to a different function of a sentence, this happens in English and Spanish as well as many other languages, without any formal training from the grammar (De la Mota 1997). Patricia Keating developed the Window model from which each phoneme has a range or threshold for frequency and formant representation, which is influenced and affected by language prosody. In other words, prosody and phonetics are not independent factors of speech production (Keating, 1999).

Syllables are just interruptions of a vocal signal. The consonant-vowel (CV) structure may not necessarily be universal, any more than a VC structure is. There may be some other factor such as how the manipulation of a vowel stream headed by a consonant may be more indicative of a linguistic production in that a vowel stream followed by a consonant. The VC may be more indicative of a nonlinguistic production. A VC syllable is just as reliably linguistic statistically speaking as the CV structure, but perceptually the CV syllable may be more salient and more readily identifiable as a linguistic structure merely due to the onset. In other words it is not so much the order in which the consonant or the vowel is produced or perceived but the relationship between the consonant and the vowel that represents the intersection of sound and language; this point marks the emergence of spoken language. By perceiving the modifications of a natural frequency produced by all typically developed people we learn to use language specific stress patterns otherwise known as language.

When the statistics do not show sensitivity towards a specific linguistic function, it may not necessarily be due to a lack of language processing. Well actually it may, but the point is that many linguistic functions do not require full activation of a grammatical structure in the brain. In other words, the gestalt of an intonation pattern may be sufficient to activate a phoneme, syllable, a word or even a phrase as well pragmatic contexts, contrastive focus, introducing new information vs old information, attitudinal and emotional expression.

The problem with most theories or models of phonological acquisition, L1 or L2, is that there are inevitably some discrepancies that cannot be explained. With SLM the problem is that categories may be impossible to attain, or the ability to discriminate phonetic categories between two languages may be reduced with age and experience. This leaves the topic of native-like L2 acquisition something of an impossible dream, yet with no explanation as to why it is impossible. The best anyone can gather is that after a certain period of physiological development a person loses more and more ability to perceive and reproduce target phonemes. So we have

Novelty of Stimulus

Novelty of experience can also explain the role of intonation in learning language. When traveling to a foreign country, our senses are filled with the sights and sounds and smells that are 'foreign' to us, but not to the natives.

For the natives of that hypothetical vacation spot, it may only be Tuesday. The novelty of experience provides exciting stimuli. It makes everything stand out as exceptional. When moving into a new house, it takes time to get accustomed to the layout, but eventually it is familiarized. It doesn't take long for us to forget about our old stimuli. This effect is so sensitive in humans that we by becoming accustomed to the amount of light or color scheme in our environments, a foreign environment's color schemes may seem heightened or pronounced in comparison to the perceptions of the natives. Soldiers' traveling back from the Middle-East will see their old faded battle dress uniforms (BDU's) as vibrant green and fresh BDU's as obnoxiously green. This is the novelty of stimulus again. The eyes had been accustomed to seeing the desert browns, and when the old uniforms are finally seen again, they are bright because the neurons are not accustomed to being registered as much by the rods in our eyes. This is also why a movie seems longer when we watch it for the first time, but gets much shorter on subsequent views. The novelty of stimulus heightens the experience. The brain learns very quickly to regard any kind of information that is attended to. In another example of the visual spectrum, soldiers who spend 12 hours using night vision goggles throughout their night watch duties will maintain the black and white color spectrum of perception for a few hours after the night vision goggles are removed. They will have less color discrimination and more "night vision." If one only one eye was used for the night vision device mounted to a helmet, the soldier will have one eye that processes black and white information, and one eye that processes their normal range of color perception. Over time the novelty wears off, and only the truly remarkable stimuli stand out. This is exactly what happens when we learn phonetics from prosodic stimuli.

The novelty of stimulus may appear to have little to do with language itself. For the sake of linguistic stress, each variation from the norm is a kind of novelty of stimulus. This initially only applies to prosody, but in languages such as Spanish and English prosodic stress indicates morphological contrasts, and even changes of syntactic mood, aside from other linguistic functions. The trick though, is that each language uses prosody in different ways to express these contrasts. It may be that since prosody has such a globalized function from biology to linguistic input that it is not truly a part of language grammar, but it still influences the processing and production within each language.

Deficiency of Input

We must not forget that external input is only part of the equation for learning a language. Interaction, which includes the input we apply to manipulate our environment as well as the navel gazing tendency we have for noticing our own interactions develops language ability. Variations in production represent differences of usage in language. Another way of thinking about this is to recall how slurred one's speech gets when tired. Certainly most people will not enunciate perfectly, or even have decent sentence structure when they have been awake for three days and they can't tell the difference between their crying baby and consoling a heavy pillow at 2:55 am. Sometimes parents are tired for decades, and maybe slurred speech is just a part of life. When it comes down to it, despite people being exhausted, drunk or just plain lazy with their articulation they are still comprehensible. The reason they are comprehensible is because prosody represents a kind of 'unwritten' grammar.

It may be that the distributional properties that regulate such utterances, without an explicit rule, is the speech stream which can indicate when and where word boundaries need to be to indicate where a subject or other part of speech should be placed. The utterance, "Who do you want'a win?" while it may sound like the use of regional dialect, it does not ring as ungrammatical. There would be an almost imperceptible pause at the end of *want* and the onset of *'a.* The difference(s) between "I wanna go" and "who do you want'a win?" may be nested deeply in the prosody. The prosody in this situation represents a similar argument of negative evidence which could be used in support of prosody as the underlying, *innate,* grammar. The pause in between the /t/ and the /a/ represent deletion of the consonant which is understood simply by a break in the rhythm of speech. It may be that such a pause is required, without being explicitly instructed, even when the utterance is produced with regional dialect which would indicate that either prosody is innate or that it is a grammatical parameter of language. Either way, in such instances the benefits of learning to flow with such language use in the ear of a second language learner is obvious. A native speaker would not even notice the missing word *"to,"* but a nonnative speaker may at best hesitate to respond, and at worst may simply shut down in confusion or exasperation. It does not take much to frustrate a psyche when speaking a foreign language.

Hyperarticulation

Making a claim for the innateness or worse, the grammaticality, of prosody does not fit within the scope of many linguist's definition systematic language. However, many studies demonstrate across various languages that prosody carries information that affect language use and acquisition across various, if not all, stages of development. This may be why our mothers, and almost anyone else who cannot resist the adorableness of a baby, use child or infant directed speech when addressing us in our earliest years of life. The ups and downs in pitch and the long drawn out cooing and the short choppy tickles make an impact on us linguistically. Using all that stimuli from acoustic information leads babies to pay more attention to all the gestures including the shape of the mouth, the appearance of the face, as well as the melody in the voice.

Anne Fernald and Patricia Kuhl, two prominent researchers who study the effects of intonation on language development, have pointed out that children respond to their native language within a few days of being born more so than they do to foreign languages. It has also been discovered that infants respond more to a female's voice than that of a male, and more to their mother's than to that of any other. When taken altogether, this research implies that either a mother tongue is passed on genetically or that it begins developing in utero. If it is developed in utero, the characteristics of language that are attended to, and which have been behaviorally researched, are the prosody and the mother's voice over all else. Perhaps the prosody of the mother's voice, and to that of the native language, raises the attention to vital details in the environment. The hyper-articulations become so deeply ingrained in us that we tend to overlook them consciously, despite their profound psychological impact.

The influence of heightened attention does not stop in infancy. Hyper-articulations are used when people flirt. Who can forget Joey from *Friends* when he asks, "How YOU doin?" Hyper-articulations also occur when people talk to the elderly, or foreigners, and even when teachers talk to their students. No explicit training has been given to anyone to address people who do not understand what is being said, but it happens all the same. Are these also innate qualities of language, or is something else going on?

Whether prosody is hardwired into an infant's language processing or it is developed by establishing connections between billions of wildly excited synapses, prosody is the source code of a language system. The best infants can do is to produce is a limited number of sounds together. They get better at it as time goes on, but in the beginning all their processing is tied up with input. They are listening, watching, feeling, tasting, and smelling everything. They use all their senses to input all the most reliable information from their environment, which we will operationally define as anything outside of their imagination, and conscious experience. This is a rather fine line.

The most basic, broken down, language specific stimuli of the in the environment are called the phonemes, and they are organized in the category that linguists call, phonetics. When these sounds become associated with a letter and that becomes a representation of the language system in the mind it is known as 'phonology.' The phonemes affect the way we produce sound in a speech stream, and since they are produced differently in isolation that in words or sentences, they are also heard differently. Even those with limited proficiency of English can tell the difference between hyper articulating the letter "A" and when the same letter is casually used in a sentence to ask someone out on a date, "Would you like to go to */schwa/* concert with me?" The difference affects the processing of speech in what researchers call, the speech stream. It may seem to be incorrect pronunciation, and therefore ungrammatical, but this slurring of speech is in fact the normal way of communicating.

How an utterance is articulated can also affect the interpretation of the intent behind the statement. For instance, before proceeding try to say, *"I don't know,"* without saying the actual words. In other words, do not use the words. Use only the intonation. If it helps, please shrug the shoulders for added effect. Now we will place that intonation into the context of a daughter asking her mother about the whereabouts of her father. When a daughter asks her mother, "When is Dad coming home?" and the mother does not lift her gaze from the book she is reading, and using only the intonation commonly used with the phrase expresses, "I don't know." The daughter understands that her mother is not listening closely or is not interested in stopping reading to answer with a complete sentence, or in some cases the utterance of three little words. However, it is enough linguistically that the mother has stated, without using the words, she does not know when the child's father will be home. All the mother must do is to hum the intonation without even saying the words. If the daughter truly needs to know, this will not satisfy her, and she may persist in questioning her mother. The mother insists, "I just TOLD YOU, I DON'T KNOW." This intonation indicates that the mother would like to be left alone. The intonation here is based off of the typical unstressed intonation patterns used in pronunciation of the words themselves, which is based on the phonetics of the letters used together to make syllables, the body's physiology, and the mother's psychological state. All of which influence the precision of articulation of the phonemes, as well as the production of the melody in the speech stream. It may be that the phrase, "I don't know," Is so common that the intonation itself has become a formulaic expression.

When it comes right down to it language learning starts with the hyper-articulated flow of intonation patterns that we learn from baby talk. Even though infants do not understand, when they see and hear actions and reactions, they will begin to mimic those actions for creative outcomes. This is not to say that they will get it right every time. They may attempt to mimic the behavior they have noticed, but they may only get close to it. They may even get creative with the language itself, making verbalizations that are at best inaccurate or maybe just a little off. When their verbal behaviors do not match up with the language that adults are using, they will not achieve their goal, whatever that may be. They may not get the toy they want, or the food source that they want etc. Eventually the little language user will get it right, and they will have their reward. This is not to say that the only reason we use language is from a behaviorist paradigm of stimulus and response. It is likely that effective communication is neurologically reinforcing whether or not the outcome of the communication is reinforcing or punishing. Our systems of communication may be reinforced by the mere fact that we expressed our intended meaning regardless of whether the interaction through language has created a reinforcing behavior or contingency from the person we are speaking with or the relationship we are developing. We may be neurologically reinforced by expressing our ideas in an argument, but actually despise the interlocutor and loathe the forced act of communication with them, or on the specific topic, which would seem to not be reinforcing behaviorally.

The act of communication may begin with babbling, and as such the reinforcement of the social ‘meeting of the minds’ as it were, would be reinforced very early on through mimesis. During the babbling phase, infants are encouraged to coo, and burble sounds creatively as well as to mimic their parents. That is, babies do not simply list off the vowels as they go to learn each one. Each phoneme is learned in relation to another. When we sit in our very first grammar class, and we already know how to speak, and listen to some extent, we learn the alphabet. Not surprisingly the vowels are often taught separately in their own set. The teacher will say, “a, e, i, o, u.” Now when the consonants are taught, they are taught in relation to at least one vowel. The first consonant in the English alphabet, “B,” is actually two phonemes that make the sound for the word “be.” The distinction is visible, but overlooked and it is audible but often disregarded. The next letter is the same way, “C” is not just one phoneme, it is the same as the first consonant but sounds more like “see.”

Elements of the mother tongue develop alongside each other to such a degree it is nearly impossible to say which is first or most important, except that without categorization of any single aspect we cannot proceed to production of language. The categorization of the phonology comes mainly from the prosodic quality, that our mothers expose us to when they are entertaining us as infants. From the hyper-articulated stress patterns we learn to isolate individual phonemes as we learn to discriminate them from other sounds by comparing their productions against the productions of other speech sounds. For instance, an "o" sounds differently when it comes before an "n" as to when it comes after an "n" in English. This is the difference between "on" and "no." The same letters are used, but the pronunciation of the vowels is different. These permutations create different frequencies in the auditory system, which have to be deciphered in order to progress linguistically in a native or second language.

It is important to be clear, so to speak. The sounds we hear and the light we see, even the odors we smell, none of those are actual sounds, colors or odors. They are all interpretations of our environment into our brains. The illusion that most people take for granted is that everyone perceives all stimuli the same. An /i/ is an /i/, and it does not sound like /e/, right? This thinking is not true. A simple explanation of this can be gleaned from people suffering from color blindness. Colorblind people cannot make out specific frequencies in the visual spectrum. Those frequencies, or colors, do not make it into their conscious awareness until they discover that they cannot see them, which could take a good while. Colorblindness is just a visual analogy to the difficulty we have in perceiving the sounds of a different language. We perceive them, but they are not being processed the same way as a native speaker does. This book's methodology attempts to counter that problem.

By focusing on the phonemes we are really getting into the specific frequencies that comprise the differences between one language's sound and those of another. The intonation patterns used in conjunction with the phonemes during baby talk heighten awareness to the phonological contrasts within a language. By producing the speech segments in a call and response exercise at the top of each page at the beginning of each class period we are giving the students an opportunity to develop full spectrum audition in the second language. This promotes phonological production and ultimately pragmatic comprehension.

Pragmatic comprehension develops through the repetitive use of the same intonations of statements and questions that express intent through the rising tones at the end of the question or the falling ones at the end of a statement. They also mark word boundaries, phrase boundaries, when it is time for one speaker to respond to another. This is true for English and Spanish, as well as many other languages, although different languages use intonation patterns in diverse ways to convey the same meanings. For example, irony has a set of prosodic features in English, and these are to some extent opposed as the prosodic features used to express irony in Cantonese (Cheang & Pell, 2008, 2009). This is yet another argument that this most basic concrete and arbitrary element of language use is not innate.

The variations possible with all the phonemes of any give language represent a daunting task to impart on a second language learner. Below are listed some of the possible variations that the manipulations of the sounds can produce, each adding not only a node, but a range or spectrum of difference for each phoneme to be contrasted with almost all others. It is important, before we continue to know exactly what we are trying to modify in the mind of the second language learner as well as the terms used to describe the phenomena.

The frequencies of a phoneme can shorten to create smaller distances between the waves. This results in a rising pitch. When the frequencies are farther apart, the result is a low pitch. Researchers from various fields (linguistics, psychology, speech pathology etc.) refer to pitch as the Fundamental frequency (F0). The amount of time a particular frequency is maintained or lengthened is called duration. The loudness with which we speak is the intensity of the wavelength, or the amplitude. Frequency, duration, and intensity perform a dance and produce other effects by the variations created between them. If one of these elements is reduced, another may lengthen. Then again, it may not. Many different permutations can be used to express different meanings, and the numbers of different meanings associated with sound (frequency) are vast to say the least.

On top of all these physical variations, we must also contend with the differences between the sexes, as well as those that come about due to age. The elderly voice has a different quality than that of a child; the oral cavity of an adult is much larger than that of a child as well (Flege, 1987). These simple physical variations affect language use, on top of the psychological influences which affect the way each age group speaks to each other. The ways a child speaks to a child, the ways an adult speaks to a child, and the ways adults speak to adults vary from within and between groups.

The biology of language development is not limited to the size of the speaker's vocal tract or the intention used when speaking. Language is not isolated from, or even far removed from all possible neurological associations with everything else going on in the world. If language use is influenced by our bodies, and our environments how then can a language's grammar exclude these functions as linguistic inputs? Because they are paired together in systematic ways, they should be included in the definition of a language's grammar. The difference between the senses being used in language is one of modality of expression. Each sensory modality is only a type of tool used to comprehend or produce language.

Prosodic Effort

John J. Ohala produced a list of biological effects that prosody has on language interpretation. Many of these sounds are said to be universal or similar across cultures. However, not all language cultures have been tested to prove this. It is simply a matter of our biology as a species and the nature of sound itself. On top of those factors the emotional factors that are so often correlated with utterances should also be universal. The effort someone uses to get our attention in one culture should not be very different from the effort used in another culture. So much can be gleaned from the effort and the biology of the speaker. Some word meanings that are often paired with language synchronically through effort and biology are as follows: size, good/bad (pleasant/unpleasant), yes/no, question/statement, emotions and attitudes. Some of the emotions and attitudes expressed through prosody are irony, humor, happiness, sadness, uncertainty, commands, requests, submissiveness, dominance, aggression etc. Smiling is even perceptible over the phone, as well as is flat affect.

A simple example of the effect language has on our senses is how we react when someone is screaming at us. Being screamed at has deep emotional implications that tell us in some way we are not satisfying some requirement. It may startle us into inaction, or even cause us to react without thinking. This is because it has activated our emotions, and all those pairings of screams that frighten us may also become somewhat activated at the same time. A man's voice can be very frightening, when it sounds sharp, loud or threatening. This is one important reason for husbands to be extremely calm and patient during arguments with their wives. The exclamation, "I'm not screaming!" is often heard from a man making a point in an argument. He may not think he was screaming, but his voice registered to the emotional centers of his partner. If the partner feels threatened, they will hardly feel comfortable.

Some limited semantic meaning can be gleaned from prosody as well as has been demonstrated by Lynne Nygaard and her colleagues in 2009. Nygaard showed this by having research participants identify nonsense word meanings by their intonations alone. From this basis of meaning, language develops. This is as close to innateness of language that can be observed. It can also explain universal nature of culture passed down to us from our parents, and most often our mothers. In this way, our mother tongue is the basis of all society, and the beginning of the differences between our cultures. Therefore it is called, "babbling," as in reference to the tower of Babel. However, this diachronic linguistic explanation is only a correlation, and is not truly causation, despite being extremely influential on our language development.

Synaesthesia

Since the size of a speaker's vocal tract, and the physical gestures used in conjunction with speech tend to amplify meaning, and since different listeners may develop non-standard sensitivities across a language group, we cannot assume that all listeners develop the same way even within a culture, let alone from a second language learning perspective. The biology associated with language, from a prosodic base, forms a synaesthetic association. Synaesthesia is the combination of the senses and symbolic information in unconventional ways to process information. A sound could be processed as a specific color, for instance. When the stimulus for sound occurs it may be connected in the brain to an unexpected sensory system. Some synaesthetes hear in color, as previously mentioned. This effect can influence language development as well, as some letters can be perceived colors as well. Prosody has synaesthetic qualities and influences with regards to language. V.S. Ramachandran and E.M Hubbard (2001) reproduced an old study that demonstrated approximately 98% of all people asked labeled a smiley face with sharp edges as probably being named "Kiki" instead of "Bouba" and the same result was found for people naming a smiley face with rounded edges as "Bouba" instead of "Kiki." This result was found regardless of socioeconomic background or native language. It has been theorized that babies may even experience synesthesia. The neurons that are associated with color may fire when they hear certain sounds. Synesthetes may feel smells, or the neurons that are associated with certain odors may activate when they experience touch. Eventually, usually, the erroneous input will be pruned away, but for some people it doesn't.

In the case of prosody, it may be that synesthesia is a default association, albeit not as exaggerated as with synesthetes who represent a statistical skew. When we listen to prosodic input from our mothers, we experience all sorts of input from our data. We have the warmth of our mother's embrace, we may be feeding, we are developing trust, learning about emotions, and developing the questioning intonations of rising tones or the declarative intonations of falling tones. Since all of this persists using intonation throughout life, there would never be an opportunity for it to be pruned away. It would be reinforced in a confusing mesh of biology, language, emotion, attitude and body language.

Synaesthetic associations in written and verbal language are evidence that the language acquisition device is not limited to what can be defined as grammar. It also calls to question what is innate, what is universal, and how could there be a poverty of stimulus when all our senses are used to engender meaning. Since it is possible for people to hear color, and to express hearing color is grammatically incorrect, the definition of language must adapt to include the extra sensory modalities. Perhaps this expanded definition can help to explain the universal components of grammar.

Learning vs. Acquisition

Learning and Acquiring a language represent different types of effort, largely based on the focus of attention vs the facilitation of attentive focus respectively. The defining factor of learning is that attention is directed for the sake of understanding incoming information. In acquisition attention is not necessarily devoted to anything in particular. This is not to say that features to be learned are not noticed, it may be that noticing during acquisition is so fast that the noticing itself goes unnoticed. When acquiring a language the attention used for a particular function, becomes unnecessary as that function becomes easier and easier to understand or produce.

Learning is different than acquiring information in many ways. Learning usually includes lesson plans, and sample sentences. Learning traditionally takes place in a classroom, or is related to education. Very often sight is the preferred modality. This can be very taxing to the brain. At least 1/3rd of the brain is set aside for the processing of visual data, according to David Eagleman a prominent neuroscience researcher. Such a large amount of processing space requires more time and resources to be assigned by the brain. This will slow down the rate of learning through visual stimuli as compared to auditory stimuli. Response times are faster in the auditory system, meaning less energy or cognitive effort is required to create neural connections. This may also represent a difference between learning and acquisition, in a sight-oriented culture.

There may be no difference in the synaptic connections, except for the locations, created by acquisition and by learning. Cell assemblies connect the same way through one modality or the other. The difference between learning and acquisition is external to the brain. In learning, the neural networks are directed by the teacher, in acquisition the neural networks may not be directed intentionally. Through acquisition, the lesson might not make sense to some, but the connections do make neuronal cell assemblies. This is not to say that the methodology of could not be used for logical instruction or that in some way by acquiring knowledge we always forget from whence it came. Much of what we learn is so mundane or repetitive that we just do not think about where we learned it, and that memory fades away with the added information and synapses being reinforced instead.

We have flashbulb memories of where we were when certain things happened in our lives. These variations from the norm represent stressful associations that stand out to us in our memories. For instance, anyone who remembers the terrorist attack on September 11th, 2001 can tell you what they were doing when they found out what had happened. Even mentioning this date here creates some cognitive dissonance in the mind of the reader, as well as the writer. This effect of stress is not isolated to emotional stress, it occurs with all variations from the norm. That is the difference between acquisition and learning.

Another explanation for the difference between acquisition and learning is that there is no basis for comparison for the acquisition of a first language and the learning of a second language. From birth to early adulthood, the "critical period" for language development starts out very strong and as we age it gets weaker and weaker. There is a plasticity, as previously mentioned, that declines over the lifespan. Plasticity from the neurological perspective is the rate at which new neurons are formed and or die off. Neurons are formed throughout life, not just while we are young, although the rate of getting new neurons does slow substantially during early adulthood. When a neuron is formed, it requires a job. If it does not get a job, it will be pruned away. It will die, and it will not come back. If a synapse does not fire for some time, it will also be pruned. When it is used in a certain way it will want to be used in that way again and again, this is how groups of similarly activated neurons form to create structures in the brain. They are assigned a task to perform; the neuron is to fire when fired upon. When a group of neurons fire together, they wire together, this is known as Hebb's Rule. In this way the critical period slowly fades away for the sake of interpreting meaning in the world.

As previously stated, the neuron does not know that it is activated or inhibited through learning or acquisition. To the neuron, it is all the same. A stimulus has been detected and that is reason enough to activate. The goal of teaching should be to facilitate the most reliable, and the most valid route to a learning objective. This approach has some opposition, mostly from those who think and feel that if learning is not difficult, it was not worth the time or effort. A common Spanish saying comes to mind that points out the ideology of most classroom instruction, "*La letra con sangre entra.*" This is roughly translated as "Learning comes from suffering." The approach of teaching pronunciation in this book is an attempt to make learning a second language as close as possible to learning the first language by using auditory forms to make listening and speaking easier for the student. Doing this creates a classroom culture; a community of smiling speaking and listening non-sufferers joined by a unifying classroom activity from beginning to end.

Some lessons we know, and have learned so long ago that we do not remember how we learned them, nor the evidence that makes them true. For instance, we do not really go about thinking why 1+1=2, we simply accept it. If asked to define what 1 means, a lay person will simply say, "What do you mean? It's 1. Don't ask stupid questions." This is far from a scientific explanation of what the number one is. In fact, research shows that we have to take a cognitive step backwards to learn addition, in that as children we already know the difference between an amount of candy and twice as much candy that goes into our siblings Halloween basket. We may not have the concept of the number 1, but we do understand the algorithm of twice as much as a certain amount without mathematical training.

The main difference between acquisition and learning from a classroom perspective is the effort which we undertook to learn the lesson. This is somewhat controversial in the context of second language acquisition. However, there is no difference between the learning in the language classroom as the learning in the science classroom. The only difference is the information being assigned to a neurological firing pattern in the brain. Our job as educators is to make that pattern as fast, true and reliable as possible under any circumstances.

When we learned our first language, we did not have the cognitive structures established that enable us to say how we learned what we learned. We barely received enough input and paid enough attention to establish the one thing we needed to remember; that being a phoneme or a new word, or a grammatically correct conjugation etc.

The difference between learning and acquisition from a neurological point of view is nil. They both create cell assemblies, they both make the same connections, and they both make future firing of those synapses easier, faster, and more reliable. Learning is the validity of formation as agreed upon by a conventional body. Acquisition is learning that may or may not be overtly agreed upon by convention, but that does not mean that it is wrong, or invalid. It simply means it may not match the academic standards of cognitive processing. Without such standards we could not assign performance ratings or grades to our students, and our entire education system would collapse, not yet anyway.

If the difference between learning and acquisition is really a reflection of how hard it was to gain the ability to use language. What makes learning so difficult, and why do we teach the way we teach? Learning is difficult because of the route we take to ensure the cell assembly reaches long term potentiation, or is stored in long term memory. As previously stated, the visual cortex requires a great deal more brain power to operate than do the other senses. With respect to language, the auditory system is much faster for adding focus to form if we consider phonetic accuracy to be a form of the target language. If anything focusing on instruction through auditory methodology concurrently with visual methodology would facilitate language learning. Most people learning a second language do not even attempt to focus on this, feeling as though it is impossible, or pointless to even come close to pronouncing the language the way native speakers do. Or perhaps they do not have the perceptual ability to discriminate between the two languages, or perhaps they feel silly or rude trying to emulate the pronunciation of another language. There is no need to feel silly or rude by trying to articulate a language in a comprehensible way, if it were rude, your mother would not have done for you as a baby. People are not rude for using baby talk, teacher talk, or foreigner talk (The elderly ***do*** consider elderspeak to be rude.) Regardless, although hyper-articulation may seem silly, the extra effort used to convey meaning comes from the speaker's desire for listener comprehension.

Some researchers claim that phonemes in a second language may be inaudible; we will call this the argument of phonological deficient perception of intake. This is very distantly related to Chomsky's argument of the poverty of stimulus. Every native speaker of a language can hears the "accent" of a nonnative speaker, even to the point of mockery. They can hear differing regional dialects, just as easily. Some people are not as accurate in their production of accents and even still some languages are more difficult to mimic for any given speaker. Since everyone can hear the difference between native and nonnative production, or two different languages, establishes that phonemes from a different language are noticeable. Noticing the difference is not enough to be able to produce a sound for oneself. This limitation most likely stems from a motor deficiency to articulate a "foreign" phoneme. Foreign is used here to express that it is not "native" but since it is at least in some way perceptible we cannot say that it is not innate. Pronunciation could therefore be an objective of a second language classroom. This is the formation of pronunciation. For people without pathological speech problems, it should be possible to at least approximate a pronunciation of a target language with minimal effort.

In society, the goodness of fit any mold determines the degree to which we are accepted as exceptional within an approved framework. Outliers to this mold, though they may have formation or "shape," of their own which may be better in some ways, but are generally not thought of in a positive light. Modifying the conventions of learning would enable the outliers to excel within the parameters of convention, and until we include everyone in our pedagogical framework, we are failing as educators. It is quite clear that some administrations are comfortable with the sacrifice.

The shapes of the sensory/motor cortex influence the ways in which we express language. It is no wonder that those who use sign language learn to do so faster than non-signers. This is due in part to the efficiency and size of brain regions devoted to processing specific types of stimuli. The somato-sensory cortex or the sensory-motor cortex has been cleverly represented by the depiction of a little man, called a homunculus, with body parts sized to represent the amount of brain matter associated with each body part. The largest areas where attention is dominant in the motor cortex are the hands in first place and the mouth and tongue in the second. There is little wonder why children using sign language learn to communicate linguistically before non-signing children, or why we learn to speak and perceive speech well before we learn to read or write. The areas sensory motor neurons associated with these regions are absurdly large and out of proportion with the rest of the body, which is rather diminutive and even a little spindly. The reason this matter with regards to language acquisition, as any deaf or blind person could tell you, is that the means of transmitting a linguistic message go hand in hand, so to speak, with the message itself. Proof of this can be easily found by asking, "Where is the "X" key on the keyboard of my computer?" If the reader raised their hands and wiggled some fingers to uncover the location of the key, they will be a part of the rest of the world that uses embodied cognition to process information. The idea being expressed here is known as "embodied cognition," and it is the contention of this paper that embodied cognition is linked with language prosody.

Our learning is tied into our bodies with as much neurological processing from that sensory input source as any other, if not more. The teaching methodology used with embodied cognition in mind is called "Total Physical Response" (TPR). It is commonly disregarded as a source of intellectual input because it is difficult to test on the GRE for example, and other modality biased standardized tests, but for the sake of teaching and learning, it is an extremely useful methodology. The amount of area associated with the motor/sensory cortex of the mouth and face indicates that these parts of the body are set up to be used efficiently. However, it seems that pedagogically we have neglected the most obvious routes for information processing in favor of that which can be graded on a sheet of paper, or bubbles to be filled in by no. 2 pencil only.

Intelligence, from this perspective, is relative to the rate of learning of the rest of people around us. If one person has a gift for learning a particular way, from visual information, then that person may prefer to learn language by writing out sentences and reading books. However, the world does not operate mostly on written language, and such students will always be lacking in some of the essential elements of a second language. Most tend to use the auditory and verbal systems for social interaction, even in the modern era. Though this may change, maybe soon, we will start dating by sitting next to each other and texting about our veal parmigiana. Despite this possibility, social interactions are still most frequently spoken and heard. Most of the mainstream world relies on auditory input for immediate processing of information, yet we do not use this processing speed in the classroom.

If we do not train the ear to hear, it will remain deaf to the sounds of a second language. Older students have more difficulty being able to describe the differences between phonemes of any language other than their mother tongue, but prosodic alignment as well as native-like pronunciation and perception are not out of the question even for adults (see Mennen, 1998).

The sounds are obviously audible, but a nonnative speaker may not be able to actually produce them accurately. It may help to think of the sounds as simply another kind of symbol or form, just like a letter. For instance, the rolling or trilled "R" of Spanish is different from the English "R." Despite being recognizable, a nonnative Spanish speaker may have trouble rolling their "R's." Each language has its own way of speaking which requires fine motor control. The fact that the motor control and the sensory system are so closely related as well as proximally located is not a great surprise. They both play a role in learning more than just how to sound like a native speaker, or hear phonemes that are foreign to one's native language, because these systems are not isolated to each other either. They are connected to the emotional systems, the higher-level cognitive systems, the hippocampal memory formations, and everything else that any individual cares to draw the connections to. Consider articulation of the phonemes of another language simply a skill instead of a cognitive task. It is a skill that will lead to faster and easier processing of cognitive tasks in any language, native or otherwise.

In teaching the phonetics and the prosody of a second language we are making the novelty of the sound system the target. The reward that is given by the acquisition of language structures will be used to facilitate other novel linguistic formations that would otherwise be limited to strict frontal lobe processing, or higher order cognitive faculties, as a function of grammar. We must decide if we want to teach second language users to communicate or if we want to teach them about the grammar of another language, and if so, what are we giving up by eliminating either one. We gain much by adding prosody into our curriculum, even if we cannot agree to accept it as integral to language itself. This is not meant as a slight or as a joke. Without the affective aspect of language in the classroom, we are limiting the second language experience to only what we accept to be knowledge of a language, with some rather blatant disregard for many sources of input that could make all the language learning easier, and more fun. Grammar and prosody are not mutually exclusive either, with facilitated use of a second language comes greater interest in the knowledge of that language.

When learning something new occurs, and is noticed, a little connection is established that will more than likely occur again. By training the ear, which is faster than the visual centers of the brain, we are motivating students to establish newer and faster connections through various modalities, not just the easily graded ones. Hyper-sensitivity to prosodic stimulus is acquired, or learned, through enough exposure and interaction. Just as anything else, however what is different about prosody is that it requires and facilitates interaction. Therefore, if the students are not getting it in the classroom, they are probably not getting it outside by doing their homework. This is probably true even with modern technology.

One way that prosody increases our ability to learn a second language is by focusing the students' attention on lexical, morphological, and contrastive stress. Stress is interpreted when we hear speaking, if emphasis on a word or a part of a word, it is that part of the word that gets focused on by most listeners. In the case of contrastive stress, we notice the differences between two versions of one utterance, and we interpret the contextual or pragmatic meaning from either. For instance, if we hear someone say, "I'm GOING!" we know that they mean business about going somewhere, but if the same words are used with stress on a different part of the utterance as in "I'M going," we focus more on the person (subject) than the fact that they are going. In the latter instance it may be that a decision has been made as to whom is 'going,' and one person has decided that they will not be left behind. In this case, the meaning is a declaration that the speaker is going. This is the kind of prosodic grammar that we learn as children, and not in a classroom. The problem for second language learners is that this scenario is never played out in the classroom, and if they can travel to a foreign country to use their second language, they will either be treated with kid gloves by the natives, or will simply be left behind; in this case both figuratively and literally. Unfortunately, it is unclear as to how much prosody affects contextual processing across languages, that is to what extent is prosody paralinguistic, and to what extent is it grammatical.

Language and Culture

We now know that language development begins at least from birth on, and that for many reasons the frequencies associated with the female voice are more pleasant, quicker to process, and we have greater access to them from motherese stimulation. Even when fatherese is the stimulus source, the same hyper articulated intonation patterns are often revealed. These patterns develop into meanings over time, eventually becoming conventional meanings which are passed down to us by our parents, and other language sources. These code sources provide the meaning we initially attend but later take for granted, even when we use the same hyper-articulated patterns for the sake of communicating with others who have trouble understanding our speech. We use these patterns with babies, with foreigners, with the elderly and sometimes with other adults to convey meanings beyond what the syntax of our sentences expresses. All these different meanings demonstrate how a culture develops first from our mother's voice, and later to whatever we want for ourselves, even to the point of developing "fighting words."

Many aspects of intonation stem from our biology and insidiously leak into our culture through language. Low tones indicate big things, and high pitch tones indicate small things. Linguistically, this carries over to language in the form of diminutives, and can also influence social interactions using nicknames, among many other things. In Spanish it is not uncommon to hear the word *mijito,* which means, "my little son." This could be used as a term of endearment or in condescension. The listener, if they are socially astute, will be able to interpret this information either now or, much to their chagrin, a few days later. However, a second language grammar class cannot teach this.

The meanings and symbols we derive from our mother's intonation patterns eventually become grammars. Each language has a grammar of phonemes which becomes the phonology. The ways words go together have a quality that makes them "legal" constructions within each language. This phenomenon is so strong that even when words are borrowed from another language, they are interpreted through the phonological system borrowing language. An example of this phenomenon in English is the word, "coyote" which is spelled exactly the same, but pronounced differently in Spanish. Even when the word is heard and not read, the pronunciation is often translated into the hearer's native language in a kind of reverse code-switching.

Meaning is shaped and determined by properties inherent in communication, which are not limited to vocal or even linguistic productions. Whichever modality is the most reliable, and is most facilitative determines the convention. Convention is the essential cultural aspect of language, and the primary method for the expression of meaning synchronically. People have developed the evolutionary need to interact with each other, as we tend to do better as a society than as isolated individuals. In order to better interact with each other and the world we have developed an ability to communicate through codes which are influenced by and reciprocally influence the cognition of individuals in our culture. The link between language and culture is derived from the conventional linguistic stimuli and responses driven by a human's need to interact with her community.

This is how we learn to use language and even to get creative with its use, by making permutations of our own for the sake of expressing new meanings. This also explains how there can be no deficiency of input. We create ungrammatical input all the time. We all make mistakes, which can catch on as new uses for language. We can also be creative with our variations of language use on purpose. If either the mistake or the purposeful creative use of language catches on with a group, it's all over. A new linguistic phenomenon can be created. If this new language form is far spread enough it will pass through an idiolect, through the regional dialect, through the cultural barriers and halls of academia, and it will be found in common parlance around the world's language. This happened with the English phrase "Okay." The term, "okay," may be the most widely used phrase in language history. It's more popular than Michael Jackson ever was, just to put the phrase's popularity into perspective. It can be heard even with present day Mayan iterations as "Octl."

Creating a Classroom Language Learning Culture

As you may have noticed, the old Spanish alphabet has been at the top of each page, but with a permutation each time. The new Spanish alphabet does not include *ch, ll,* or *rr.* The changes in the order of the alphabet are purposeful. Producing the sounds of the language from A to Z is all fine and good, but does not duplicate the linguistic gymnastics that are required for articulation or comprehension of speech. Pronouncing the letters as closely to the native pronunciation as possible at the beginning of class, and asking the students to simply mimic the instructor as closely as possible, can help students in several ways.

Performing this alphabet ritual helps each individual attempt to produce and perceive the language at the same speed and rhythm of the instructor. The instructor must also make the sounds, so the students will have an example to mimic. When the students hear the instructor performing this task, they will learn the rhythm of the instructors' idiolect. If the instructor is a native speaker of the target language, the students will naturally attempt to follow along. This worked well in our Spanish classes for a few different reasons, chiefly among them is that at first glance, I am nothing more than a Anglo-American with blond hair, and blue eyes. There is nothing particularly "Spanish Speaking" about me, which may allow students to feel that they too can speak Spanish well. The idea is that "If this white man can do it, surely I can too." If nothing else, this can create a classroom culture as well as a classroom accent, if everyone really gets into it. The performance of this task initially allows the students to produce target language sounds as closely as possible without having to focus on the meaning, which may detract from their cognitive processing of the phonemes themselves. It also can be very fun, and as such will lighten the mood of the classroom, by allowing the students and the teacher to psychologically prepare for the second language experience. Stephen Krashen proposes that second language learners suffer from an "affective filter," which severely limits activation of the language acquisition device. This teaching method is based on the assumption that the affective filter reduces the motivation and agency of second language learners by keeping them from fully participating with another language in a new way. Therefore, by assigning this task to students at the beginning of class everyone can practice together, and everyone can fail together. It is even good for them to see and hear the professor have difficulty from time to time, so that they do not judge themselves too harshly. It is also beneficial for the students to see the non-native speaker performing well so they can be more critical of their production efforts.

When the prosody and phonotactics of speech are learned or acquired by the students, they will be able to process the information faster than they did before. In this way learning to pronounce and comprehend the language by interacting with it helps comprehension at all other stages of language learning. Performing this task develops phonological categories in the minds of the students so that they may process second language information faster and with greater ease. This is as close to the critical period as we can get, and it may be the key factor in developing native like prosodic competence, which eventually leads to improved pragmatic competence.

Babbling or, "motherese" can help to develop a second language identity or language ego and influences acculturation through the appropriation of a native like accent (Flege 1987). Instead of a mother tongue, which they already have, they can create a sister tongue. They can even choose the accent they would like to produce. If any student wishes to mimic an accent, they can bring that accent to the classroom. The teacher can also provide examples of diverse cultural methods for pronouncing different phonetic speech samples from Argentina, Paraguay, Cuba, Spain etc. They could even get as specific as using the accent from the Yucatan peninsula, for instance.

The cost of not developing this area means that at best second language students will have to settle for non-native like comprehension and production of second language intonation. They may never be able to tell a joke in their second language or even worse, they may never truly understand a joke in their second language. At worst they will fill the ranks of people who once took a language in school, but have mostly forgotten how to use it. If this method can access the parts of our first language that innately cause us to process language in the way that we do our native language, students may be able to retain more of their one or two Spanish classes for longer periods of time.

To use this methodology combine the phonemes into ever increasing difficulties of pronunciation, as have been given at the top of each page in this article. Eventually students will be able to easily process the sound systems, and their affective filter will drop. They will feel much more confident in their speech, as well as their comprehension. Foreigners will be surprised when they hear a non-native speaker using native like pronunciation. The concerted effort to reach the target audience on the same "wavelength" goes a long way, and they are usually happy to interact. With obviously struggling second language learners, native speakers often must either slow down by using foreigner talk, or put extra effort into the communicative process with the second language learner. If the effort becomes too great, they native speaker may abandon the attempt altogether, or may even attempt to speak to the second language learner in their target language. The latter scenario happens all the time for native English speakers, as more and more people are influenced by the world wide spread of English. Anything that can be done to facilitate the interactions between language users should be a goal of the language classroom.

In a second language classroom it can be difficult to create an environment that maximizes learning in that the language barrier between the teacher and the students is hopefully as vast as or larger than the distance between a tourist and a native, or a college math professor and their undergraduates. The teacher may hyper-articulate using a sound system that is foreign to the students. The students, not really wanting to pay attention in the first place, may struggle to follow along due to the alien sounds coming from their teacher's face sounding like noise. In an effort to reduce the noise, facilitate the possibility for attentive focus, and reduce the cognitive load required to learn a second language teaching the sound system of the language without any semantic meaning can have impressive pedagogical results.

Focusing on pronunciation has received some support in the classroom, but many teachers lack the patience, or the perceptual ability to correct a student's mispronunciations. Many students and teachers feel that it is irrelevant to try to produce the sounds of a second language accepting that a non-native like accent is simply something second language learners will have to deal with forever. Others have abandoned the task altogether citing theories about sensitive periods which indicate that the ultimate attainment of a second language very rarely means sounding like a native-speaker. These theories disregard the benefits of developing a perceptual sensitivity in the target language at early stages, instead favoring to focus on semantic meaning or grammatical structures which are, of course, essential. These fields are not without their obvious merit, in that they are required in order to speak the target language well. However, learning the sound system early on in the developmental process brings various benefits.

Christine Moon and her colleagues propose that when a newborn hears their mother's voice, their attention fixates on the sound and the gestures even *in utero*. After birth the infants attend to their mother's voice and of their native language in a unique way than they do foreign languages and the spoken words of people who are not their mothers. This may be the basis of the phrase, "Mother tongue." By learning the sound system of the second language we are attempting to replicate a child's sensitivity to their mother's speech by training the ear of an adult. This is no small task, but it is may not be as impossible as we have been led to believe. The respected linguist Richard Schmidt proposes that by raising awareness of any aspect of language will increase the likelihood that the given aspect will be attended to upon future exposures. This theory falls in line with theories proposed by Christine Moon & and many others regarding first language acquisition; that by raising awareness of the forms to be associated with functional meaning in a second language we can heighten the attention of our students and enable them to more easily perceive the sounds that will be seemingly bombarding them with stimuli at a much different rhythm, and "frequency." This literally puts the language learners on the same wavelength through which they can learn to segment speech which will enable them to identify phrase boundaries which indicate that a thought has been fully expressed, or when it trails off among many other unacknowledged linguistic phenomena. By becoming sensitive to the target language prosody and phonetics the learner can develop an appropriate perceptual and productive ability which will compound exponentially allowing for attention to be raised in the following areas: pronunciation, intonation, rhythm, voice onset timing, morphological, semantic, syntactic, and pragmatic use and comprehension. However, many language teachers, and researchers have imposed outdated limitations on the language learning communities by stating past a certain age or sensitive period a student will not be able to acquire native-like production in a second language, and therefore the effort should not even be made until students are obviously more serious about the second language.

Another benefit that this method carries is a reduction in teacher talk. The language barrier is one of the most obvious hindrances to the second language classroom. Many teachers avoid this problem by speaking in the non-target language in the classroom. Doing this severely limits the opportunities the students have for exposure and interaction with the target language. The classroom is one of the only places our students have access to their target language, so the class time is of utmost importance. Another way of getting around the language barrier is by slowing down the speech pattern, and using what is known as 'teacher talk.' It is interesting that this happens almost naturally, without the teacher being aware that it is happening. They are trying to naturally make it easier for the students to listen, and to understand. This phenomenon is not particular to teachers either, almost everyone does it. Native citizens of a language culture use the same technique when speaking to foreigners. We use different rhythms and speech patterns when we are speaking to people outside of our age group; both older in the case of elderspeak, and younger in the cases of child or infant directed speech. Unfortunately slowing down the speech patterns severely limits the students', or listeners', affordances to parse information at the rate of speed they will be expected to understand in the real world. The problem is that by speeding up, the students will be unable to maintain focus, or even attend in the first place. In order to close the gap between the student and teacher we must meet in the middle somewhere. We must make it easier for the student to hear what we want to teach without having to limit the input they will receive. This can be accomplished simply by practicing the sound system itself, as though it were a grammatical structure and a learning objective in the curriculum, as well as by always speaking and being spoken to in the target language in the classroom.

Taking a somewhat bold leap from the pedagogy back to the theory, this methodology was created from a rejection of the proposal of a poverty of stimulus. Let us propose, for the sake of argument that there is no poverty of stimulus. In contrast, let us assume that the richness of stimulus is too vast for statistical or behavioral measure from a linguistic perspective. The innateness of language could be the very human need to see or create meaningful patterns in almost everything they take in through the senses. The difficulty in measurement lies in the multi-modal avenues through which we begin to sense the world. Stimuli that engender meaning can be embodied initially, through synaesthetic connections, sensitized and habituated gradually in order to be replaced by conventionally reliable and even abstract meanings in order to input ideas that are not in our umwelt. This happens in order to reach a common ground with ideas outside from our own perceived reality. Language is not only created through the pairing of meaning and sound, or externalization, initially, but meaning and as many senses as we can associate to the meaning in order to express an idea. Eventually most of the methods used to express an idea are whittled down in order to fit the mold used by the majority of society. From the pruning of the unconventional, and therefore less reinforced and less reliable, systems for pairing meaning to symbol, natural language emerges. The biologically encoded synapses create what are the initial sense interpretations of non-arbitrary meaning, which eventually develop into arbitrary meanings. However, those earlier connections are not disregarded in their totality; they persist in a regressive state. In other words, the baby is not thrown out with the bathwater, and sometimes the baby is not even completely dried off. Any approach to language that disregards all the internal properties that create consciousness and are responsible for the emergence of language itself, is missing the underlying principle of natural language which is the ability to express idea from a global consciousness through conventional means, whether those means are concrete or abstract, arbitrary or non-arbitrary. The sensory experience paired with language is not ancillary, it is essential in order for expression, and ideation, to meet with convention. Language does not begin at one particular point; it is consistently developed and modified through use within a community.

The fact that synaesthetic, and prosodic embodied connections exits, and that by these connections we learn what a sharp sound or a rounded sound is like, we are then able to take the idea of sharpness or roundedness and apply it to other structures, actions, or ideas. Language comes in as a shared, therefore conventional, experience of systematic concrete to abstract meaning all from the pairings of external stimuli to ideas that are statistically more than likely to be shared by a group of people.

The opposite view to this connectionist model is that ideas are in some way innate, and that linguistic representations are later added on to them in order to exchange ideas through language symbols. The innateness of language does not account for synesthesia nor does it allow for concrete form to function relationships. Language must be arbitrary and abstract in order for the poverty of stimulus to be fully valid. The innateness of language may stem from concrete relationships that are built upon creatively to what becomes prescriptively and conventionally included into the definition of language proper. The idea expressed in this book, and the methodology for developing linguistic representations in a second language Spanish classroom, is that an idea can be imagined creatively or input by the environment. Ultimately this means that the mind has to interpret what the environment has to offer. If there is not language to describe a tube to someone that does not mean the person cannot imagine a tube, and how such a shape could be used to siphon a fluid from one area to the next.

Innateness of linguistic representation as ideas in the mind does not allow for creativity or the imagination to be the innate aspect of language which takes a concrete sound and functional meaning and makes that same idea an abstract inference to be shared by a community. Language, could in that instance, then be the systematic conventional abstraction of perceived concrete pairings to external stimuli with cognitive activity. This abstraction of concrete associations is the critical point in support of this teaching method, whether it successfully changes the definition of language or not. The arbitrariness of language stems from the conceptualization, or the inference from associations of concrete meanings to external stimuli. It is the relationship that defines the abstract relationship, not the symbol or the meaning. The leap from concrete form to abstract thought is as simple as thinking about the sharp edges of the name "Kiki" and carrying that idea of sharpness to another symbol such as a finely cut diamond. This leap is as far away from the phonetic /k/, but the idea that sharpness and sound ever coincided is still a part of our language development. The sharpness would still be identified robustly and conventionally as "kiki" when the options are presented. The sharpness of the sound is yet another verbal symbol associated with the sharpness of an object, and the idea persists and creative permutations of the meaning will coincide with the shape again. Think of it as simply another word, that while it may not have grammatical applications in a sentence, it still influences parsing. A language's phonology, phonotactics, and prosody also influences language acquisition directly, and continue to influence language use and therefore have a definite role to play in the second language classroom.

Language may be the relationship between the concrete and the abstract. It does not rest in the symbol nor in the mind, but in the necessary interaction between the two, which is conventionally shared to a statistically significant degree. The farther removed from this significance probably can represent actual social distance in the real world. This is what this teaching method attempts to revive and resolve for the second language learner, to refresh the language learning or acquisition processes all over again.

Some theorists claim that it is the merging of two systems, of phonetic categories, that enables native-like production. This little book and methodology propose that by establishing separated phonological representations and by subsequently developing compartmentalized linguistic systems, we are able to develop a new sound system from the prosody all the way to the pragmatic competence.

By developing target language prosody and phonetic ability, we will be able to consider or disregard all the nuances of communication that we do in our first language. We may be able to quickly comprehend ironic or sarcastic utterances while disregarding the more grammatical semantic meanings taught in a second language classroom. This is a kind of Gestalt Language learning system, instead of a rote memorization system.

Student Evaluations of Instruction:

"Around halfway through the semester I was talking with Mr. Baird and he asked me "Why don't people enjoy my class?" I said something like, 'Look, you're teaching Spanish 103 to a bunch of (mostly freshman) students who are only in here because they have to be. Intro to Spanish is dull subject matter. Maybe out there there's some genius of a teacher who makes Spanish 103 fun, but I doubt it.' But after that the classroom experience started to become more and more fun. We began learning more during class while legitimately enjoying our time there. I don't know how he did it, be he has made almost every student in that class look forward to MWF Spanish class. I always liked him as a teacher, and he has earned my complete respect."

"The best!!! If I had this instructor for 101, I would have been better prepared for 102. I actually began to understand a little Spanish."

"Made me understand Spanish and taught in the most interesting ways."

"His teaching style and the time that he took to make sure his students were actually learning the language made me make the decision to minor in Spanish."

"Understands language very well. Innovative teaching methods, but they work. Class was actually fun. I enjoyed going to class and learning."

"He is the best professor ever and I believe I learned more Spanish in a month than in 2 years of taking it in high school. He also made the class extremely fun and he made you want to come to class."

"Learned more in his Spanish class than any other Spanish class I've ever taken."

"Baird strives to create a positive and enjoyable learning environment, without sacrificing learning."

"I recommend this course to anyone wanting to learn Spanish. At the beginning it might feel like you're not learning anything, but later during the class you find just how much you have improved!"

Bibliography:

Cataño, L. Barlow, J. A., Moyna, M. I., (2009) A retrospective study of phonetic inventory complexity in acquisition of Spanish: Implications for phonological universals. *Clinical Linguistic Phonology.* **23**(6), 446-472. doi:10.1080/02699200902839l8.

Cheang, H., & Pell, M. D.,(2008) The sound of sarcasm. *Speech Communication* 5, 366-381.

Cheang H.S., & Pell, M.D. (2009) Acoustic markers of sarcasm in Cantonese and English. *Journal of the Acoustical Society of America.* **126** (3), 0001-4966/2009/126(3)/1394/12/$25.00.

Cho. T. & Keating, P. (2009) Effects of initial position versus prominence in English. *Journal of Phonetics.* 37, 466-485.

Chomsky, N. (2012) Poverty of Stimulus: Unfinished Business. *Studies in Chinese Linguistics,* Vol. 33, Number 1. 3-16.

Dupoux. E., Pallier, C., Sebastian, N. Mehler., (1997) A Destressing "Deafness" in French? *Journal of Memory and Language,* 36, 406-421.

Eagleman, D. (2015) The Brain: The Story of You. Vintage Books.

Fernald, A. & Kuhl, P. (1987). Acoustic determinants of infant preference for motherese speech. Infant Behavior and Development 10.279-293.

Fikkert, P. (1994) On the Acquisition of Prosodic Structure. Holland Academic Graphics. The Hague.

Flege, J.E., (1987) A critical period for learning to pronounce foreign languages?, Applied Linguistics, 8, p.162

Gass., S., & Selinker, L., (2008) *Second Language Acquisition 3rd. ed.* Routledge: U.K.

Gutiérrez Díez, F. (2001). The Acquisition of English Syllalbe Timing by Native Spanish Speakers Learners of English. An Empirical Study. *International Journal of English Studies.* Vol. 1 (1), pp. 93-113.

Imada, T., Zhang, Y., Cheour, M., Taulu, S., Ahonen., & Kuhl, P. (2006). Infant speech perception activates Broca's area: a developmental magnetoencephalography study. *Brain Imaging: NeuroReport.* Vol. 17. No 10. July.

Krashen, S. (1985) *The Input Hypothesis: Issues and Implications.* Longman Inc. New York.

Keating, P. (2006). Phonetic Encoding of Prosodic Structure: *Speech Production: Models, phonetic processes, and techniques,* 167-186.

Kuhl, P.K. (2010) Retrieved 11/10/17: Brain Mechanisms in Early Language Acquisition.
https://www.ncbi.nlm.nih.gov/pmc/articles/PMC2947444/#!po=11.5672

Lavoie, L. (2002). Subphonemic and Suballophonic Consonant Variation: The Role of the Phoneme Inventory. *ZAS Papers in Linguistics* 28, 2002, 39-54.

Levi, S. V. & Schwartz, R. G. (2013) The Development of Language-Specific and Language Independent Talker Processing. *Journal of Speech Language Hearing Resolution.* 56(3): 913-920. doi: 10.1044/1092-4388(2012)/12-0095).

Meisel, J.M., (2011) First and Second Language Acquisition. Cambridge University Press.

Mennen, I., (1998). Second language acquisition of intonation: the case of peak alignment.

Moon, C., Lagecrantz, H., Kuhl, P. (2013) Language experienced *in utero* affects vowel perception after birth: a two-country study. *Acta Paediatr.* 102(2): 156-160. Doi: 10.11111/apa.12098

Nygaard, L., Herold, D., Namy, L. L., (2009). The Semantics of Prosody: Acoustic and Perceptual Evidence of Prosodic Correlates to Word Meaning. *Cognitive Science* **33**, 127-146. DOI: 10.1111/j.1551-6709.2008.01007.x

Ohala. J. J., (1984) Cross-language use of pitch: An ethological view. *Phonetica* **40**, 1-18.

Ramachandran, V. S. & Hubbard, E. M. (2001). Synaesthesia—A Window Into Perception, Thought and Language. *Journal of Consciousness Studies,* **8,** No. 12, pp. 3-34.

Ramus. F., Nespor, M., Mehler, J. (1999). Correlates of linguistic rhythm in the speech signal. *Cognition.*

Schmidt, R. (1993) Awareness and Second Language Acquisition. *Annual Review of Applied Linguistics* **13,** 206-226. Cambridge University Press 0267-1905/93.

Vitevitch, M.S., & Stamer. M. K., (2006). The curious case of competition in Spanish speech production. *Language Cognitive Process.* 21(6): 760-770. doi:10.1080/016909605000287196.

A ch H E G – J K Z S C – R rr D T L – ll Y ñ U O – P W B V F – N I M Q D

Appendix: Some other iterations of the Spanish alphabet. Please do not constrain your approach to using this method by these configurations or even by these separations of five letters in six groups. Mix it up as much as you like, and in a way that will benefit each day's lesson and objectives.

C Z G J H – ll R L rr ñ – T D P B W – V F Y A I – N E M X ch – Q O U K S

A E I O U – F S N M ll – C K Z T B – V ch X D P – Q G H rr W – J L R ñ Y

C P T I S – X E K ñ V – D M B rr U – F Y G J ll – H R N L A – ch Q O W Z

D I M Q U – Z ch H ll P – T Y C G L – O S X B F – K ñ rr W A – E J N R V

A E J N R – V B F K ñ – rr W L G C – O S X ch h – ll P T Y D – I M Q U Z

D I A ll C – Z E N rr T – O P K Q U – V X R ch M - W Y J G H – F B S ñ L